THE BODY *and* THE BLOOD

THE BODY *and* THE BLOOD
THE POWER OF COMMUNION

The Believer's Practical Guide to Personal Partaking

LAVONNE BAKER

ETCETERA PRESS LLC
Richland, WA
2013

PUBLISHED BY ETCETERA PRESS LLC

Copyright © 2013 by Lavonne Baker

The Body and the Blood: The Power of Communion
The Believer's Practical Guide to Personal Partaking

Printed and bound in the United States of America by Etcetera Press LLC, Richland, WA.
www.etcpress.net

All rights reserved. No portion of this book may be reproduced in any form or by any means, including information storage and retrieval systems, without written permission from the publisher, except by a reviewer, who may quote brief passages in a review.

ISBN: 978-1-936824-18-2
Library of Congress Control Number: 2012941825

In this publication, pronouns referring to God, Jesus Christ, and the Holy Spirit (i.e. He, His, Him) are capitalized for reading clarity. Also, the word "blood" is capitalized when referring to the Blood of Christ.

Unless otherwise noted, all Scripture quotations are from the *King James Version* of the Holy Bible.

Scripture quotations marked (NIV) are taken from the *Holy Bible, New International Version*. Copyright ©1973, 1978, 1984 by International Bible Society. Used by permission of Zondervan Publishing House.

Scripture quotations marked (NLT) are taken from the *Holy Bible, New Living Translation*, copyright ©1996, 2004. Used by permission of Tyndale House Publishers, Inc., Wheaton, Illinois 60189. All rights reserved.

Scripture quotations marked (TLB) are taken from *The Living Bible*, ©1971. Used by permission of Tyndale House Publishers, Inc. Wheaton, Illinois 60189. All rights reserved.

Scripture quotations marked (AMP) are taken from *The Amplified Bible*, Copyright ©1954, 1958, 1962, 1964, 1965, 1987 by The Lockman Foundation. All rights reserved. Used by permission. (www.Lockman.org).

Scripture quotations marked (NKJV) are taken from the *New King James Version*. Copyright ©1982 by Thomas Nelson, Inc. Used by permission. All rights reserved.

Contents

Acknowledgements *viii*
Foreword *x*
Introduction *xiii*

The First Step

1. Discerning the Lord's Body *1*

Believers Can Partake of Communion to

2. Remember the Covenant We Have With God *7*
3. Receive the Salvation / Healing Package *13*
4. Energize and Revive Our Souls *19*
5. Replenish After a Cleansing Session *23*
6. Draw Near to God When Our Fellowship With Him Has Been Broken *27*
7. Lay Hold of What is Provided for Us In Jesus Christ *37*
8. Worship the Lord Our God *43*
9. Offer Thanksgiving to the Lord and Honor His Precious Blood *49*
10. Be Raised Up and Restored *53*
11. Intercede For Others *59*
12. Fellowship With One Another *67*

Epilogue *73*
Salvation Prayer *75*
Author Note Of Transparency *79*
About the Author *81*

Acknowledgements

First and foremost, Thank You Heavenly Father, for orchestrating and sanctioning this Project, and for allowing me to experience what is written on these pages; Thank You Jesus Christ, my King, and Lord, and Glorious Saviour, who this book is meant to honor and exemplify. *I love You Lord. IT'S ALL ABOUT YOU!*

Thank you to my Family: to my Mother and best friend, Lavern, for your unrelenting belief in me, for your never-ending love, encouragement, nurturing, and serving, and for all the years of fervent intercession for me (and countless others); to my sisters, Teresa and Kathryn, for your abounding love, generous prayers, and your ongoing support in life, and for this Project; to my niece Jami and your lovely family for your love and for the much-needed times of fun and laughter; to my late earthly father, Fred, a remarkable wordsmith and expositor, from whom I inherited a great love for words and their meanings; and to my late twin sister L. Negesti whose quiet strength, selflessness, and profound courage continue to inspire me. *I love every one of you and thank God for you.*

Thank you to my sister in Christ and life-long prayer partner, Pastor Shirley Conley (Rivers of Glory Christian Center, Pasco, Washington) for your unwavering commitment to God and true friendship; to Corinne Keith (Publisher of the Personal Promise Bible*) for your friendship, and for your diligent, dedicated review of this Project; to Terry Cupples, Bessie Garza, Karen Campbell, Marielena Mendoza, and all my friends and co-workers for your prayers and encouraging words throughout this endeavor. *You are all very much loved and appreciated.*

Last, but not by any means least, thank You Gracious, Long-suffering Holy Spirit for entrusting me with this Project, and empowering and equipping me to put it together. Thank You for Your continual Presence, and for the Rhema promise of Zechariah 4:6-9. Spirit of Christ, never, ever could this have been accomplished without You. *I absolutely love You.*

* http://www.personalpromisebible.com

Foreword

One of the many glorious blessings of being a child of God is the wonderful privilege of participating in Communion: the meaningful, purposeful partaking of the elements that represent the Body and the Blood of Jesus Christ. In His wisdom and great, immeasurable love for us, God has instituted and given us this practice, and He has designed it to be a mutual, give-and-take transaction between us and Him. He has saturated it (Communion) with tremendous power, and He longs for us to discover and experience all that is available to us when we partake.

The intricacies of Communion are great, but it is by simple faith that we believe and receive its manifold provisions. Although the exercise of Communion itself is packed with power, God has ordained simple elements, bread and wine (cracker and juice), to be used for this purpose, and

He counts them holy and significant when they are set apart unto Him.

When we partake of Communion, we symbolically receive Jesus Christ who is the very bridge and connection between us and Almighty God. This Jesus Christ-connection unites us with God who is the supreme source of all love, life, light, peace, healing, joy, hope, cleansing, wisdom, forgiveness, prosperity, power, protection, and provision. This union by way of Communion is available to us at all times to address areas of need in our lives or in the lives of others, or simply to tap into the sheer, incomparable joy of fellowshipping with the Father and basking in His holy, magnificent presence. The reality and pleasure of having such unrestricted access to God is what makes Communion so very special to me.

The purpose of this book is to share with others what the Holy Spirit of God has revealed to me about the Body and the Blood of Jesus Christ, and the incredible power of Communion. My hopes and prayers are that you will be encouraged to participate often in Communion, that you will discover and experience its many wonderful provisions, and that, as a result, you will be lifted to a new and greater level of fellowship and intimacy with God our Father.

Nothing written herein is intended to imply that taking Communion solves all our problems and makes them go away. However the intent is to convey that when we set aside time to come before the Lord, acknowledge, honor, and worship Him, then respectfully receive the elements that represent His sacrificed Body and Blood, our focus is put back on Him, and the cares and concerns of this life become secondary and less important. That's the way God expects us to live.

May the powerful, embracing Presence of the Holy Spirit be with you as you study and put to practice these valuable truths.

> *"For my flesh is meat indeed, and my Blood is drink indeed." ~ John 6:55.*

Introduction

Many people think of Communion as an "at-church" event where believers gather and partake together of the Lord's Table. God certainly blesses this time of assembling and fellowship, but every believer in Jesus Christ needs to know that Communion can also be a "one-on-one-with-God" activity. Taking Communion privately and individually is a special privilege that many children of God may not know they have.

Webster's Universal Unabridged Dictionary lists the following definitions of the word *Communion*:

1. Fellowship
2. Intercourse between two or three persons
3. Interchange of thoughts or interests
4. A state of giving and receiving
5. Agreement, concord

Clearly God's plan for Communion is to have a time of intimate sharing and powerful exchange between Himself and His people. Communion is a two-way line of communication which allows the action of giving and receiving to take place between God and us. It allows us to touch Him and be touched by Him in return, which makes it so appropriate, then, to include Communion in our private times alone with Him.

This book focuses on implementing the power of the Body and the Blood of Jesus Christ to address the many diverse issues of our lives. Life's issues can, of course, be presented to God without the partaking of Communion, but I believe this book will show you a more excellent way. Communion allows us to activate and draw on the very power of the Body and the Blood of Jesus Christ for whatever we have need of. I have found that including Communion in my personal prayer time intensifies my awareness of Jesus Christ (who He is and what He has done), deepens my love for Him, and applies His very Presence and victory to the situation I'm praying for.

There are several different terminologies used for the partaking of the Body and Blood of Jesus Christ. The most common are:

Communion	Holy Communion
The Lord's Table	The Lord's Supper
The Eucharist	The Sacrament

Each of these terms identify the time we set aside to honor our Savior and partake of the elements that represent His broken body and shed Blood. It's a time to remember the sacrifice that He made to purchase our salvation, cleanse us from sin, and reconcile us back to the Father.

It is important to know and remember that our Communion elements are ***symbols only*** of Jesus Christ and the sacrifice He made for mankind. Receiving these elements demonstrates our faith in what He did for us on the Cross, and activates in us its power and provisions.

As you read through this book, you will notice that each chapter includes or ends with a brief instruction or a sample prayer for taking Communion for the subject discussed. These are guidelines only. As you develop in this practice, you will find that the Holy Spirit will give you prayers and words to speak for your own personal situations.

Note: Although this book is written with the focus on Communion, one other subject is intended to be illustrated and hopefully stands out loud and clear, and that is: ***the importance of time alone with God.***

Every child of God has been given the privilege to have a deep fellowship and intimacy with the Father, but this rich, fulfilling oneness with Him must be individually pursued and appropriated. Time alone in His Presence, prayer, studying and meditating on the Word, praise, worship, and Communion, all done consistently, lead us into a wonderful intimacy with God, and into the fullness and depth of joy that He created us to have with Him.

Jesus taught in Matthew 6:1-18 that giving, prayer, and fasting are all best done in private, in our quiet place alone with God. The message here is that God puts great value on our time alone with Him, and so should we. Time alone with God is absolutely vital for victorious living. No earnest time spent in the Presence of God goes unnoticed, unacknowledged, or unanswered by Him.

One

The First Step:
DISCERNING THE LORD'S BODY

The Bible emphasizes the importance of discerning the Lord's Body prior to receiving Communion. I Corinthians 11:28-30 says,

> *"But let a man examine himself, and so let him eat of that bread, and drink of that cup. For he that eats and drinks unworthily, eats and drinks damnation to himself, not discerning the Lord's body. For this cause many are weak and sickly among you, and many sleep."*

Two key words in this passage are **unworthily** and **discerning**. Webster defines them as follows:

Unworthily: *irreverently, lacking respect*

Discern: *to understand, perceive, recognize mentally, detect*

By these definitions we see that we are to respect and reverence the exercise of Communion and the One it represents. We are to have the fullest understanding possible of the Lord's Body and His Blood. Discerning the Lord's Body is a serious matter to God and He warns us that death can result for not heeding this instruction. This chapter explains why this is so important to Him.

God's Redemption Plan

In the beginning when God's first man--Adam--sinned, the fellowship and union between God and mankind was completely severed. Adam's disobedience cut man off from his relationship with God, and disconnected him from God's heavenly, spiritual realm. Every person born from that time on carried the sinful nature of Adam and was inherently separated from God. The severance between God and man would have remained <u>forever</u> unless the debt for that first sin was paid. By God's own law, payment for sin had to be death (***"For the wages of sin is death…" Romans 6:23***), and furthermore, payment had to come from someone who was without blemish, someone who had never sinned. No human being was totally faultless, and animal sacrifices could only temporarily cover man's sins. God Himself was the only being who could meet His own requirement for a perfect, sinless specimen to represent mankind. Therefore, in order for man's debt to be paid and for the gap to be closed between man and God, God Himself would have to die. The value God placed on mankind was high enough that He chose to take man's place in death for payment of his sins. I John 3:16 reads,

> *"Hereby perceive we the love of God, because He laid down His life for us ... "*

Titus 3:4-7 (NIV) reads,

> *"But when the kindness and love of God our Savior appeared, he saved us, not because of righteous things we had done, but because of his mercy ... "*

Now, in order for God to take man's place in death, He had to fully identify with man; He had to *become* a man. So, as stated in John 1:1 and 14, God became flesh.

> *"In the beginning was the Word, and the Word was with God, and the Word was God."* v. 14 *"And the Word was made flesh, and dwelt among us ... "*

God Himself came from heaven and took on human form, and we know Him in this human form as Jesus Christ. In Matthew 1:23 He is called Emmanuel, God with us. Colossians 2:9 (TLB) says,

"For in Christ there is all of God in a human body…"

Jesus Christ was the physical manifestation of God in the flesh, on the earth. He was the fulfillment of God's desire to abide with, provide for, and redeem mankind… His most precious creation.

Through Jesus, God taught and fed the multitudes, healed the sick, raised the dead, and received all who would receive Him. Jesus Christ was God in the flesh, walking with, talking with, touching, and loving mankind. Then the time arrived for God to carry out what He had come to earth to do. When Jesus Christ was crucified on the cross, it was God Himself on that cross, paying the price for all men's sin. It was God, through Jesus Christ, who died, was buried, and was resurrected to carry out and accomplish His own perfect plan of salvation and redemption for mankind. No other death would have been sufficient; no other blood could have purged and washed away the sin of mankind. Second Corinthians 5:18 and 19 (AMP) read,

"But all things are from God, Who through Jesus Christ reconciled us to Himself [received us into favor, brought us into harmony with Himself] …" v. 19 "It was God [personally present] in Christ, reconciling and restoring the world to favor with Himself…"

God's entire Redemption Plan for mankind was founded upon His own incarnation and sacrifice. It was Almighty God, the Creator of all heaven and earth, who stepped out of His place of glory and clothed Himself in mortal flesh, all to rescue a sin-sick humanity from death, and restore them to Himself.

This is why God requires and commands us to earnestly consider and discern the Lord's Body. He came to earth, lived, suffered, and died in that body, and gave it as a ransom for all mankind. Every human being *owes* it to Him to honor, reverence, and respect His Body and Blood to the utmost, highest degree!

Discerning the Lord's Body

Discerning the Lord's Body at Communion is much more than just remembering that Jesus died on the cross for us. To discern the Lord's Body is to understand the truth about Jesus Christ, that He IS God; God Himself manifested in the flesh, demonstrating His tremendous, incomprehensible love for us, and giving His all to pay for our sins and reunite us with Himself. JESUS CHRIST IS GOD, and it is Him, His Body, and His Blood that we celebrate in our times of Communion. Jesus' own words are recorded in I Corinthians 11:24-26:

> *"... Take, eat: this is My body which is broken for you: this do in remembrance of Me. ... This cup is the new testament in My Blood: this do you, as often as you drink it, in remembrance of Me.... For as often as you eat this bread, and drink this cup, you do show the Lord's death till He come."*

When we partake of Communion, we are to reverence and honor our Lord God, and recognize and understand who He is and all He has done. We are to acknowledge and proclaim His glorious sacrifice on our behalf until He comes again to take us Home.

Conclusion

There are no limits or restrictions on how often we can or should partake of Communion, but whenever we do, it's important that we make sure our partaking is not mechanical or ritual. As often as we eat and drink, we are to do so respectfully, and in deliberate, purposeful discernment and remembrance of Jesus Christ, and His Body and Blood.

Two

Believers Can Partake of Communion to:

REMEMBER THE COVENANT WE HAVE WITH GOD

Since the beginning (Genesis 1) and all throughout history, God has established covenants with mankind. Because of Adam's sin, man through the ages has been continually entangled in adverse situations, and God has continually intervened by way of covenants and agreements to rescue, protect, provide for, and sustain him. These various covenants addressed God's instructions, laws, and promises to mankind. They demonstrated the immutable, unshakable faithfulness of God, His willingness to care for His people, and His determination to accomplish the final, remarkable work of reconciling mankind back to Himself. This was a long process, but it has been ultimately accomplished in Jesus Christ. There are seven main covenants recorded in Old Testament Scripture:

God's First Covenant with Man – Genesis 1

God's Covenant with Adam – Genesis 3

God's Covenant with Noah – Genesis 9

God's Covenant with Abraham – Genesis 15

God's Covenant with Moses – Exodus 19

God's Covenant with His people Israel – Deuteronomy 29, 30

God's Covenant with David – Samuel 7

Our New Covenant

As God's people, we too have a covenant with Him. Our Covenant with God is a blood covenant, initiated by the Blood of Jesus Christ. Hebrews 9:16 and 17 explain that in order for a will (a testament) to go into effect, the testator (the one who leaves the will) must die. Jesus fulfilled this requirement when He died on the cross to pay the price of man's sin. His shed Blood was the result and proof of His death, and it was the exact element needed to set in motion the will, the testament, of God. Our covenant with God was authorized and executed by the death and the Blood of Jesus Christ. Speaking of Christ and His Blood sacrifice, Hebrews 9:15 says:

> *"And for this cause He is the mediator (negotiator) of the New Testament, that by means of (His) death, ...they which are called might receive the promise of eternal inheritance."*
> (Words in parenthesis added for clarity)

Our Covenant, the **New Testament** (or New Covenant), addresses every area of our lives and provides everything we need. The New Testament is the written documentation of all that has been provided for us through Jesus Christ. God's Word, promises, and provisions are activated and established in our lives by the Blood of Jesus Christ. Every promise belongs to us, and is accessible by faith.

Our Blood Covenant with God has provided us with:

- Total payment for and forgiveness of sin
- A restored relationship with God as our Father
- Citizenship in the Kingdom of God
- Oneness and unity with God through Jesus Christ
- The Spirit of God living inside of us
- Unlimited access to the heavenly realm of God
- Freedom from the bondage and dominion of sin
- Spiritual weapons that promote our victory in life

- Restoration to God's Presence, protection, provision, and prosperity
- Eternal, everlasting life

In our Blood Covenant with God, His promises to us and provisions for us are full and complete, therefore, as His people, our lives and destinies can be full and complete. Second Peter 1:3 (NIV) reads,

> *"His divine power has given us everything we need for life and godliness … "*

Ephesians 1:3 declares,

> *"Blessed be the God and Father of our Lord Jesus Christ, who has blessed us with all spiritual blessings in heavenly places in Christ!"*

Our Blood Covenant has it all!

As believers, we have the privilege of spending time in fellowship with God, confessing His promises, and meditating on the Covenant we have with Him. We can take Communion during this time to activate and celebrate His promises, and be uplifted, strengthened, and encouraged. It pleases God when we acknowledge and rehearse our Covenant, and it helps us remain focused on Him and walk in the awareness of His Presence, His love, and His total provision for our lives.

Three

Believers Can Partake of Communion to:

RECEIVE THE SALVATION/ HEALING PACKAGE

Strong's Concordance Old and New Testament definitions of the words Saviour, Save, and Salvation provide powerful illustrations of who Jesus is, and what He has provided.

Old Testament Definitions:

Saviour: reference #3467 Yasha: *"Avenging"*, *"defend"*, *"deliverer"*, *"help"*, *"preserve"*, *"rescue"*, *"be safe"*, *"bring salvation"*, *"save"*, *"get victory"*

Save: reference #3467 Yasha: Same as above

Salvation: reference #3444 Yeshuwah (which is JESUS in Hebrew): *"Deliverance", "health", "help", "salvation", "save", "saving/health", "welfare"*

New Testament Definitions:

Saviour: reference #4990 Soter: *"God or Christ", "Saviour"*

Save: reference #4982 Sozo: *"Heal", "preserve", "save", "do well", "make whole"*

Salvation: reference #4991 Soteria: *"Deliver", "health", "salvation", "save", "saving"*

Jesus Christ *is* God The Saviour, and He has provided both salvation and healing for us in one grand package.

Salvation

God made it clear in His Word that only blood could atone for or pay the price for sin. In the Old Testament, the blood of animal sacrifices–once a year–was sufficient to stay God's hand of punishment for man's sin. Leviticus 17:11 reads,

> *"For the life of the flesh is in the blood: and I have given it to you upon the altar to make an atonement for your souls: for it is the blood that makes an atonement for the soul."*

In the New Testament, the sacrifice of the shed Blood of Jesus Christ–once and for all–fulfilled that requirement. Hebrews 9:22 and 28 (NIV) reads,

> *"... and without shedding of blood there is no forgiveness." v. 28 "... so Christ was sacrificed once to take away the sins of many people ... "*

Ephesians 1:7 says (speaking of Jesus),

> *"In whom we have redemption through His Blood, the forgiveness of sins ... "*

And Revelation 1:5b reads,

> *"Unto Him that loved us and washed us from our sins in His own Blood ... "*

When Jesus Christ was beaten and hung on the cross, His side was pierced, His Blood spilled out, and He died. His Blood was pure, holy, and full of the divine life and power of God, and it was everything that was needed to pay for all men's sins, forever. Because the price was paid, God now allows every person who comes to Him by that precious Blood to be fully reconciled to Himself. Our Blood-bought salvation includes:

>Redemption – Ephesians 1:7, Colossians 1:14, I Peter 1:18, 19

Forgiveness – Ephesians 1:7, Colossians 1:14, Hebrews 9:22

Justification – Romans 5:9

Cleansing – I John 1:7, Hebrews 9:14

Sanctification – Hebrews 13:12

Peace with God – Colossians 1:20

Access to God – Ephesians 2:13, Hebrews 10:19

Victory over the enemy – Revelation 12:11

Because of the Blood of Jesus Christ, salvation for mankind is available and complete, and these provisions and benefits belong to all who will believe.

Healing

The sacrifice of the Body of Jesus Christ also purchased our healing. I Peter 2:24 says,

> *"Who His own self bare our sins in His own body on the tree, that we, being dead to sins, should live unto righteousness: by whose stripes you were healed."*

On the cross, Jesus suffered outwardly from brutal beatings and horrible physical pain to bare and absorb all sickness and disease for mankind. He suffered inwardly with undeserved rejection, ridicule, and humiliation to take on man's inward pain, grief, and sorrow. Every bacteria and virus, every mental and bodily malady and malfunction was laid upon Him. With His body mangled and ripped apart, all the sin, sickness, disease, and depravity of the entire world and the very curse of death itself were fixed upon Him, all at the same time. Jesus was afflicted with such extensive abuse and torture that it appeared that He was being punished for committing the most brutal and unspeakable acts imaginable. Isaiah 53:4 and 5 read,

> *"Surely He hath borne our griefs, and carried our sorrows: yet we did esteem Him stricken, smitten of God, and afflicted (as if He Himself was a vile, horrible sinner).* **But** *(the truth is),* **He was wounded for <u>our</u> transgressions, He was bruised for <u>our</u> iniquities: the chastisement of <u>our</u> peace was upon Him, and with His stripes <u>we</u> are healed."*
> (Words in parentheses added for clarity.)

So much damage and destruction did Jesus Christ sustain that His Body was gnarled and distorted beyond recognition of even being human! The Bible says in Isaiah 52:14 (NIV),

> *"… his appearance was so disfigured beyond that of any man and his form marred beyond human likeness…"*

Healing was purchased for us when Jesus Christ sacrificed His own Body and Blood and died in our place.

God wants us to understand the significance of the Body and Blood sacrifice of Jesus Christ, and the impact it has on our lives today. He wants us to know that Christ's substitionary sacrifice freed us from the dominion of sin (and all its results) and the bondage of sickness. By the shedding of His Blood, we are saved. By His bruised and beaten Body, we are healed. The total salvation/healing package was signed, sealed, and delivered to mankind when Jesus Christ died and rose again. In all His sacrifice and suffering, He left *nothing* unfinished. The crucifixion, death, burial, and resurrection of Christ has resulted in total provision for every area of our lives. Our salvation and healing are complete.

In this time of Communion, partake of the bread and the cup to acknowledge and remember the Lord's complete package of salvation and healing, and to set in motion the power and deliverance it provides for you. Take a stand on God's Word, and give thanks that His promises and provisions are for you! Jesus Christ is our salvation and healing. He gave His Body and Blood, each with their own objective and purpose, so that we could have abundant life. Communion time is a perfect time to receive by faith the results of His generous giving.

Four

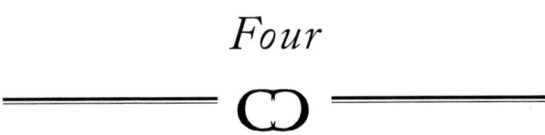

Believers Can Partake of Communion to:

ENERGIZE AND REVIVE OUR SOULS

Throughout our lives, every one of us will face challenges and battles which will tire us out, weigh us down, and even destroy us if we allow them to. Without a doubt, in this world we will all have "opportunities" to become weary and discouraged. Discouragement and weariness result when we allow our focus on problems or circumstances to be greater than our focus on the reality of God and His faithfulness to keep His promises. Because He never intended for us to be weary or weighed down, God has given us several ways that we can be energized, lifted up, and revitalized. When situations seem overwhelming and discouragement tries to set in, we need to make a willful, determined effort to fix our eyes on Him and His promises. Psalm 42:5 reads,

> *"Why art thou cast down, O my soul? and why art thou disquieted in me? hope thou in God: for I shall yet praise Him for the help of His countenance."*

Psalm 61:1 and 2 read,

> *"Hear my cry, O God; attend unto my prayer. From the end of the earth will I cry unto thee, when my heart is overwhelmed: lead me to the rock that is higher than I."*

We must remember that God is our source of encouragement and victory, and it is from Him that we receive strength and the ability to go on. Taking Communion can play a large part in reviving us and getting us back on track.

Jesus spoke in John 6:53-56 saying,

> *"Verily, verily I say unto you, Except you eat the flesh of the son of man, and drink His Blood, you have no life in you. Whoso eats My flesh and drinks My Blood has eternal <u>life</u>: and I will raise him up at the last day. For My flesh is meat indeed and My blood is drink indeed. He that eats My flesh and drinks My blood <u>dwells</u> in me, and I in him."*

Jesus said that those who eat His flesh and drink His Blood have eternal, everlasting life, and they dwell in Him, and He in them. The "life" He speaks of is 'zoe' life, the divine, heavenly, Kingdom-life that comes only from God. The word "dwells" means to remain in a given place, to abide, to be present, to continue in. Jesus is instructing us that His divine life and Presence exist continually with and in those who partake of His Body and Blood. God Himself takes up residence in us and fills us with His Life and continual Presence.

Jesus Christ gave His life so we could abide in Him and Him in us, in all times, good and bad. Understanding the reality of His indwelling presence lifts us high above the weight of our circumstances, out of discouragement and into the hope and power of His promises. With the knowledge of this truth in our hearts and minds, we don't ever have to feel weighed down or overwhelmed by circumstances. The Resurrected Savior is alive in us, and we can draw from the well of His zoe life and refreshing any time we need to. We can dismiss weariness and step into His strength and vitality. We can let go of depression and rise up into His valiance and endurance. We can dispel heaviness with the Word of Truth and live victoriously with Him!

We have the zoe life and Presence of Almighty God residing continually in us. When we keep our eyes on the Lord, and our thoughts and words on His promises, hopelessness or discouragement will have no place in our lives. When we remember who resides in us, that "give-up" spirit cannot come near us. God lives in us to strengthen and energize us, and to enable us to live above our circumstances.

Partaking of Communion for this cause will help get your focus off of your battles and despairing circumstances, and back onto Jesus Christ. When you partake, do so with the remembrance of Him, that He is your life, your strength, your encouragement, and your "lifting up" in every situation. Speak out loud the truth of His promises and faithfulness to you. Remembering the truth of who He is in you will strengthen and fortify you, and drive out every thought or feeling of defeat. Let this Communion be a time of revival, refreshing and rising up out of discouragement into the place of victory and soundness that is ours in Christ Jesus.

Additional Scripture References

Psalm 28:7	I Corinthians 2:9
Psalm 33:18-22	Ephesians 5:18-20
Isaiah 51:11	II Corinthians 2:14
Hebrews 4:14-16	Philippians 4:6-9
	Galatians 6:9

Five

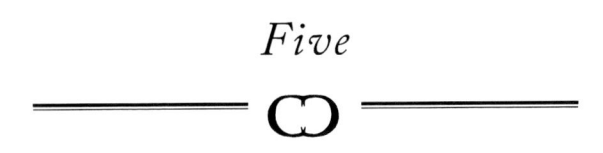

Believers Can Partake of Communion to:

REPLENISH AFTER A CLEANSING SESSION

Most of us have spent time before God in heartrending prayer sessions, i.e. times when we go to God to pour out our heart, and confess hurts, disappointments, anger, bitterness, unforgiveness, and hidden resentments towards others. We present to God the painful hurts and rejections that we have harbored inside, sometimes for years, and allow Him to help us release and forgive those who caused the pain. Anyone who has experienced this kind of purging and emptying out knows that the emotional and physical drain can be tremendous. In times like these, we need a way to fill up again, to be replenished with something from God. Communion is the perfect way. Communion allows us to replace that which has been expelled and removed, with the wholeness and fullness of God.

Harboring bitterness, anger, hurt or unforgiveness inside can manifest in our lives in destructive ways and adversely affect our health and overall well-being. It distracts us from the things of God, and impedes the working of His perfect will in our lives. God requires us to let go of hurts and wounds, old and new. He commands us to forgive so our hearts can be pure and our walk with Him unhindered. Scripture is clear about God's view of unforgiveness. Psalm 66:18 says,

> *"If I regard iniquity in my heart, the Lord will not hear me."*

Mark 11:25 and 26 read,

> *"And when you stand praying, forgive, if you have ought against any: that your Father also which is in heaven may forgive you your trespasses. But if you do not forgive, neither will your Father which is in heaven forgive your trespasses."*

Matthew 6:14 (NIV) says,

> *For if you forgive men when they sin against you, your heavenly Father will also forgive you. But if you do not forgive men their sins, your Father will not forgive your sins."*

God is very aware of the distress and anguish that can come from everyday living, and from revisiting painful events and memories from the past. He, too, has experienced human-ness and all the trials, difficulties, and "un-fairnesses" that occur. The Bible says in Hebrews 4:15 (NIV),

> *"For we do not have a high priest who is unable to sympathize with our weakness ... "*

God Himself lives inside of us, therefore He feels what we feel, and hurts when we hurt.

Since God *requires* us to forgive and let go of bitterness and anger, He also *enables* us to do so. He is with us through the process of relinquishing and cleansing, and He will help us through the rending and wresting that sometimes takes place during these times. Then, once we let go of the harmful baggage, Jesus can reach into those areas of our innermost being which were once laden with anger and unforgiveness, wash away the hurt and pain, pour in His peace and comfort, and raise us up cleansed and whole from the inside out. Jesus Christ is our true Healing Balm. Psalm 138:3 says,

> *"In the day when I cried thou answered me, and strengthened me with strength in my soul."*

When you partake of Communion to deal with unforgiveness and past issues, remember Jesus Christ who is the Master Healer of every hurt and wound, past, present, and future. As you partake of the Communion elements, ask Him to come in and fill up those places left empty when you released hurt and bitterness, the places now cleansed by your confession and forgiveness of others. Recognize that the Communion elements represent the full measure of Jesus Christ and all who He is, and receive that fullness as you partake. Allow Him to surround you, fill you, and minister His healing and wholeness to you. You can then begin to live in the freedom that comes with releasing others from the bonds of bitterness. When you let go of hurts and resentments, the Holy Spirit can flow freely through you and enable you to rise up and fulfill God's perfect plan in your life.

Six

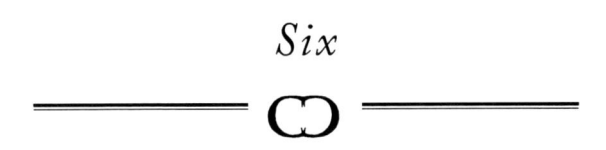

Believers Can Partake of Communion to:

DRAW NEAR TO GOD WHEN OUR FELLOWSHIP WITH HIM HAS BEEN BROKEN

The Bible makes it clear that it is God's plan and desire to have intimate fellowship and communication with His people. Our Father finds much pleasure in our company, and by His design we receive power and ability for victorious living when we abide continually in Him. Jesus Christ is our example of life lived in absolute fellowship with the Father. He lived in conscious connection to the Father in the spiritual realm, and He functioned from that realm to carry out God's plan in the physical, earthly realm. Because He purposefully stayed connected to the Father, Jesus lived, moved, and operated at all times in the very center of God's perfect will, and in all the fullness of His power.

God intends for us also to experience and live this divinely-connected lifestyle, but we may sometimes allow things into our lives that interfere with our fellowship with Him. As a result we slip out of intimacy with God and away from the awareness of His Presence and His divine realm. Sin, disobedience, busy-ness, slothfulness, and misaligned priorities can break our fellowship with God and rob us of being consciously connected to Him. God has however, because of His great love for us, given us the partaking of Communion that we may draw close to Him once again.

God's relentless pursuit of fellowship and intimacy with the human race can be seen, not only in His incarnation and sacrifice, but also by examining the work and ministry of the Blood of Jesus Christ. God has made the Blood of Jesus to be a powerful disinfectant and coagulant that works unceasingly to connect mankind to Himself. The Blood of Jesus:

- made redemption available to mankind and sanctifies the redeemed unto God,

- paid the price for all men's sins and restored his access to God,

- cleanses every repentant sinner and allows him to abide in God's presence,

- justifies man before God and gives him personal, intimate access to Him.

The Blood of Jesus Christ connects man to God, period, and it is the only element that could accomplish this. Colossians 1:19-22 in the NLT reads,

> *"For God in all his fullness was pleased to live in Christ, and through him God reconciled everything to himself. He made peace with everything in heaven and on earth by means of Christ's blood on the cross. This includes you.... You were his enemies, separated from him by your evil thoughts and actions. Yet now he has reconciled you to himself through the death of Christ in his physical body. As a result, he has brought you into his own presence, and you are holy and blameless as you stand before him without a single fault."*

It is by the Blood that we have peace with (access to, union with) God.

Hebrews 10:19 says,

> *"Having therefore, brethren, boldness to enter into the holiest by the Blood of Jesus ... "*

By the Blood of Jesus, we are allowed into even the most holy place of God. Ephesians 2:13 reads,

> *But now in Christ you who sometimes were far off are made nigh by the Blood of Christ."*

Strong's Concordance in the New Testament Greek helps give a full picture of the meaning of this verse:

> The word *far*, reference #3112, is makran, which means *"at a distance"* or *"a great way off."*

> The word *made*, reference #1096, is ginomai, defined as *"to cause to be"* or *"to become."*

> The word *nigh*, reference #1451, is eggus, a verb meaning *"to squeeze near"* or *"to draw near."*

> From the word *nigh* in the Concordance, we are directed to reference #43, the word *agkale*, which means *"a curved arm."*

When these simple definitions are assembled, we see a beautiful message emerge:

> **"Now in Christ, you who were once a great way off (from God) are caused to be squeezed near by the Blood of Christ."**

Or, more completely,

> **"You who were once distant from God are now in Christ Jesus, and His Blood (like a curved arm around you) draws you near."**

What awesome power in the Blood of Jesus Christ, and what a glorious picture of the tender, accepting love of Almighty God! God wants us near Him, and by the Blood of

Jesus Christ, He receives us right into His sweet, holy Presence with pure, total, unconditional love.

God accepts the shed Blood of Jesus Christ on man's behalf, and by it He allows all who will to come to Him. No relationship with or access to God is possible without the wonderful, powerful, life-giving Blood of Jesus.

When our fellowship with the Father is broken, we need only to confess and turn from our wrongdoing with a sincere heart. I John 1:7 and 9 tell us that the Blood of Jesus washes away all uncleanness. These Scriptures read,

> "… *and the Blood of Jesus Christ His Son cleanses us from all sin." v.9 "If we confess our sins, He is faithful and just to forgive us our sins, and to cleanse us from all unrighteousness.*"

For this particular occasion of Communion, purpose to spend extra time in prayer and in the Father's Presence. Once you have confessed your sins and received His forgiveness, focus on His love for you and all that was sacrificed to allow you access to and intimate fellowship with Him. When you receive the bread, remember and honor our Lord Jesus Christ who gave His whole spirit, soul, and body to give us life, and to reconcile us back to the Father. Receive the cup in remembrance of Him whose precious, powerful Blood gives us peace with God and escorts us right into His holy Presence. Let the Blood of Jesus draw you near, into the loving arms of God the Father. He longs to receive us and hold us close, and He generously pours out His love on us when we take time to draw near to Him.

When we stay in continual fellowship with God, we will stay consciously connected to Him, and we will live like Jesus lived--full of power from God's spiritual, heavenly realm, and operating on earth in the center of His perfect, holy will.

A Call to Repentance

Even after experiencing the reality and power of ongoing, long-term fellowship and intimacy with God, it is possible for a believer to break that fellowship, stray away from God, and remain disconnected from Him for days, months, and even years. Those in that state merely exist from day to day. Fellowship and intimacy with God, and power from above are no longer a part of their lives. They become carnal and uninspired, all the while quenching the call and bidding of the Holy Spirit, and ignoring their inner longing to return to fellowship with the Father. If this describes your present condition, you need to know that God loves you with a powerful, unconditional, everlasting love, and although your ***fellowship with*** Him may have been broken, your ***relationship to*** Him remains unchanged. You are still His dearly loved child, and He longs to be in fellowship and communion with you again.

In the Old Testament, God spoke loving, inviting promises to His people who were disconnected from and out of fellowship with Him. In Isaiah 55:1-3 (NLT) God says,

> *"Is anyone thirsty? Come and drink—even if you have no money! Come, take your choice of wine or milk—it's all free! Why spend your money on food that does not give you strength? Why pay for food that does you no good? Listen to me, and you will eat what is good. You will enjoy the finest food. Come to me with your ears wide open. Listen, and you will find life. I will make an everlasting covenant with you. I will give you all the unfailing love I promised to David."*

In 2 Chronicles 7:14 He promised,

> *"If My people, which are called by My name, shall humble themselves, and pray, and seek My face, and turn from their wicked ways; then will I hear from heaven, and will forgive their sin, and will heal their land."*

In Jeremiah 29:11-14a, God says,

> *"For I know the thoughts that I think toward you, saith the LORD, thoughts of peace, and not of evil, to give you an expected end. Then shall you call upon Me, and you shall go and*

pray unto Me and I will hearken unto you. And you shall seek Me, and find Me, when you shall search for Me with all your heart. And I will be found of you saith the LORD ... "

These same promises are intended for you today, right now, right where you are. No matter how long your separation from God, and regardless of the cause, Father God is waiting for you to come back to Him. When you call earnestly upon Him, the Blood of Jesus Christ is available to cleanse you from all sin and uncleanness, remove every schism between you and the Father, and restore you into full fellowship with Him once again. Praise God for His mercy! The miraculous Blood of Jesus Christ gives you total access to the Father, and your fellowship and communion with Him can be completely restored.

Instruction and Exhortation

Discipline and the commitment to spend quality time in the Father's Presence are absolutely necessary to re-establish the intimacy you once had with Him. Abundant time in the Word, and diligent, "press-in" prayer are essential in order to purge your heart and mind of unclean, worldly debris, and fill them up again with the pure and holy things of God. It takes time, too, to consciously re-connect with God, and to become tangibly aware again of His divine Presence. Whatever is required, however long it takes, it is important to not become frustrated or discouraged during the process. Remember that it takes time to develop *true* intimacy in *any* relationship. Be persistent in your pursuit of God. He is not a sinister taskmaster who makes us beg or perform to enter into His Presence. He is our loving heavenly Father who truly wants us near and in fellowship with Him, and He will joyfully receive you and draw you in to His Presence again if you will earnestly seek Him.

Also, remember that you have an adversary that wants to keep you separated from God and void of the joy and power that comes from abiding in His Presence. Resist his attempts to make you feel undeserving or doubtful of God's love, and stand against him by speaking God's Word when thoughts of defeat or unworthiness come to mind.

God's loving arms are open wide to receive you right now. Let today be the day that you turn your heart back to Him and begin to be restored into the fellowship and intimacy that He intended, and that your heart (and His) longs for.

Seven

Believers Can Partake of Communion to:

LAY HOLD OF WHAT IS PROVIDED FOR US IN JESUS CHRIST

The many names of God are recorded in Scripture to reveal to us His awesome magnitude and His extraordinary, unlimited power. God's wonderful names are the promises of His provisions and the pictures of His glory. The revelation of them is our permission (and invitation!) to know Him intimately by His names, and to address Him accordingly. This chapter presents Communion as a time to call upon the name(s) of the Lord to *receive something from Him*. The following chapter also offers Communion as a time to acknowledge the Lord by name, but for the purpose of *giving something back* to Him.

Jesus Christ is the very fulfillment of all the names of God. Jesus *is* God. He is Emmanuel, God with us, and all the power, attributes, and provisions of God are wholly contained in Him. Since we symbolically receive Jesus Christ when we partake of Communion, what better time than then to address Him by His name(s), and lay hold of what is provided for us *in* that name? Jesus is:

Jehovah Jireh	The Lord our Provider	Geneis 22:14
Jehovah Rapha	The Lord our Healer	Exodus 15:26
Jehovah Nissi	The Lord our Victory, Banner	Exodus 17:15
Jehovah M'Kaddesh	The Lord Who sanctifies us	Exodus 31:13
Jehovah Shalom	The Lord our Peace	Judges 6:24
Jehovah Sabaoth	The Lord of Hosts	I Samuel 1:3
Jehovah Rohe	The Lord our Shepherd	Psalm 23:1
Jehovah Gaal	The Lord our Redeemer	Isaiah 49:26
Jehovah Tsidkenu	The Lord our Righteousness	Jeremiah 23:6
Jehovah Shammah	The Lord who is Present with us	Ezekiel 48:35

God's Names are given to us so that we can know and experience all that He has for us. At Communion, we can call on *any* name of the Lord and lay hold of the promises and provisions that are contained in that name:

For healing we can pray:

> "Lord God, You are Jehovah Rapha, the Lord my Healer. Your Name reveals that You are the treatment, the remedy, and the cure for every malady of spirit, soul, and body. I thank You, Lord, that as I receive these elements that represent Your Body and Your Blood, I receive You. When I receive You, I receive the healing that You provided for me. Thank You Jesus, for you are Jehovah Rapha, the Lord my Healer."

We can call on Jehovah Rohe and pray:

> "Jehovah Rohe, The Lord my Shepherd, thank You that I am Your child, and You call me by name. I know Your voice and follow You. I acknowledge You, Great Shepherd, as I partake of Communion today, and I open my ears and my heart to hear and receive Your instruction and wisdom. I place my trust in You, and thank You for lighting my path by Your Word. Thank You for loving me, residing in

me, and guiding and directing me in the way I should go."

We can ask for and receive God's peace:

"Lord Jesus Christ, as I bow before You to partake of these Communion elements, I do so in remembrance of You. I thank You that You are Jehovah Shalom, the God of all peace, and You are The Lord my Peace. Thank You that You sacrificed Your life on the cross to purchase peace for me. The punishment that brought me peace was upon You. As I receive these elements that represent You, Jehovah Shalom, I receive Your provisions of peace, wholeness, and soundness into every area of my life."

The promises and provisions of God are not limited to His "Jehovah" Names. He is also:

Our Strength and Power	2 Samuel 22:33
Our Maker who gives songs in the night	Job 35:10
Our Rock and our Fortress	Psalm 31:3

A Shield, our Glory, and the Lifter up of our head	Psalm 3:3
A very present Help in trouble	Psalm 46:1
A Shelter for us	Psalm 61:3
Our Defense	Psalm 89:18
Our Hiding Place	Psalm 119:114
The Father of Mercies, and the God of all comfort	2 Corinthians 1:3
The God of all grace	I Peter 5:10

God's Names reveal His plan, desire, and ability to meet our every possible need. He is ***everything*** to us, and He wants us to call on Him in every situation. Relying on The Lord, and calling on His Name as we receive Communion is our point of contact for focusing on Him, and laying hold of His never-ending provisions.

Eight

Believers Can Partake of Communion to:

WORSHIP THE LORD OUR GOD

The Names of God in *this* chapter are listed, not for us to focus on *what He has provided* for us, but that we may see and understand the greatness and glory of *who He is*, and respond to Him in WORSHIP.

As believers, we *belong* to God; we are His beloved and purchased possession. We have received the gift of new life in and by Him, and we have been given direct access to His Holy, glorious throne. God has made us kings and priests unto Himself (Revelations 1:6), and our absolute charge is to reverence and worship Him accordingly.

Webster's Dictionary defines worship as a *heart* response:
> To reverence with supreme respect and veneration
> To have intense love or adoration for

To respect, to honor

To have unbounded admiration for

Strong's Concordance describes worship as a *physical* response:

To bow oneself

To fall down flat, to prostrate oneself

To make obeisance

To reverence

These definitions illustrate the heartfelt, willful, and physical submission of one, to love, honor, and reverence another; in this case--our worship of God. Our worship is to be both *an action*, and *an overall lifestyle*, dedicated to loving, honoring, and yielding to Almighty God.

The names of God describe His excellent, sovereign character *and* His attitude and passion toward us. Our God and Savior is the Creator of the Universe, the Redeemer of all mankind. He is the Alpha and Omega, and the God who was, and is, and always will be. Jesus is the Conqueror of sin and death, the saving God who accepted us, cleansed us, and gave us citizenship in His divine, heavenly Kingdom. He is:

Elohim	The Supreme God	Genesis 1:1, 24:3
El Elyown	The Most High God	Genesis 14:18
El Shaddai	The Almighty God	Genesis 17:1
El Olam	The Everlasting God	Genesis 21:33
El Qadowsh	The Holy God	Joshua 24:19

He is:

El Roi	The Seeing God	Gen 16:13
El Aman	Faithful, Steadfast, Sure God	Deu 7:9
Elpelet	The Delivering God	Psalm 18:2
Elchanan	The Gracious God	Ps 116:5
El Gibhor	The Mighty God	Isaiah 9:6

There are many more names of God given to us in Scripture, but these few alone give us more than enough reason to live our lives worshipping Him. When we see His names, which demonstrate His glory, strength, majesty, and unconditional love and faithfulness towards us, how can we respond to Him with anything less than worship? God is worthy of worship, and worshipping Him is our calling, our assignment, and our duty.

The Power of Worship

The *action* of worship is powerful and effective, and we are strengthened and matured as we stay loyal to honor and minister to God:

- Worship requires us to purposefully set aside our feelings and circumstances, and choose to focus on *who* God is. Our willingness and obedience to worship Him even in difficult times reveals what we truly believe about Him in the depths of our soul, and demonstrates our true level of commitment to Him.

- Worship keeps the issues of our lives in proper perspective, and enables us to endure the trials and difficulties of this world. It helps us live above our earthly circumstances, and stay connected to the One who is and has the answer for all of life.

- Worship transports us right into the Presence of God. When we enter into true worship, God responds to us by drawing us unto Himself, and allowing us to experience His majesty and glorious Presence. He holds nothing back of Himself when we worship Him with a pure, sincere, focused heart.

- Worship satisfies a strong God-given desire to know and commune with Him, our very Maker. We were created and put on this earth to worship God, and in worshipping Him, the true purpose for our life and existence is realized and fulfilled.

Worship may well be the most intimate and passionate part of our communication with God. There is no higher calling, no holier place than before Him in true worship. Every believer would greatly benefit from regularly and often holding a private session of on-purpose, heartfelt worship unto God. John 4:23 says,

> *" ... But the hour cometh, and now is, when the true worshippers shall worship the Father in spirit and in truth: for the Father seeks such to worship Him."*

God looks for, loves, and deserves our worship. Choose today to be one who is consistent and faithful to give Him the worship and honor that He is so worthy of.

For your Worship and Communion session, begin to honor and thank God for *WHO* He is (not necessarily because of *what* He has done). Acknowledge who He is by speaking His Names and attributes back to Him. Include in your worship bowing and kneeling before Him, singing, lifting holy hands, and absolutely embracing Him with love and adoration.

> "Lord, You are The Creator and Possessor of all heaven and earth. You are the Holy, Majestic, High and Lofty God, The Glorious God, The God of all Gods, and The God of all Love and Truth. Lord, You are Good and Upright, clothed with Majesty. You are The Excellent One, The King of Glory, Great in Power and Mighty in works! You are Almighty God, The Fountain of Living Waters, The King of all nations. You are The True God, The Living God, The Everlasting King!

You are my Savior and Deliverer, my Rescuer from death and hell. You are The God of all Mercy and Compassion, the Source and Giver of Life itself. You are God with the Master Plan for my life on earth and for all eternity. I worship You, El Olam, my Everlasting Savior. I worship You Gracious, Faithful God, my Victorious Redeemer! You are the God of Peace and the God of Hope. The God of all Comfort, The God of all Grace. You are the Only Wise God, the Glorious, Shining God, The First and The Last! You are He who lives forever and ever. Lord, there is no one like You!"

At the end of your time of loving and worshipping God and exalting His Name, receive your Communion elements with thanksgiving, honoring and praising Him for who He is. Use this opportunity to commend your life to Him, for during times of worship more than ever, you will become more aware of Him, and of your obligation (and privilege) to commit your whole life and being to Him.

Nine

Believers Can Partake of Communion to:

OFFER THANKSGIVING TO THE LORD AND HONOR HIS PRECIOUS BLOOD

Everything Jesus did while on this earth was to meet the needs of others, and to point them to God. His crucifixion, death, burial, and resurrection were for the service of all mankind. Jesus' own words in Luke 22:19 and 20 are:

> "... *This is My body which is given for you; ... This cup is the new testament in my blood, which is shed for you.*"

For all He has done for us, Jesus Christ deserves our thanksgiving in return. Every person owes Him generous thanks for His remarkable gift of Eternal Life. His sacrifice cost Him everything He had, and our offerings of thanksgiving show our gratitude to Him, and give Him the recognition He is so worthy of.

In addition to our thanksgiving, we should also take time to honor and celebrate His powerful, life-giving Blood. The Blood of Jesus Christ is holy and pure, and it carries the Life of God Himself. His Blood is Divine, the only one of its kind, which makes it precious, priceless, and fitting to be held in the highest esteem.

An earlier chapter states that "our Covenant with God was authorized and executed by the death and the Blood of Jesus Christ." Jesus' Blood set our Covenant with God in motion. God's benefits, blessings, and promises are ours by Christ's Blood alone. Acknowledging, contemplating, and honoring this Precious Blood is, without a doubt, our reasonable service.

At Communion time and always, our thanksgiving to Jesus Christ and the honoring of His precious Blood should flow freely from our hearts:

> "Lord Jesus, I come before You to celebrate *You*, and to receive this Communion in remembrance of You. Thank You for dying to give me Life. Thank You for the promises of God that are mine because of You. Thank You Lord for Your love, for Your sacrifice, and for the relationship I have with God because of You. You are The Truth, Lord Jesus, and I thank You for manifesting Yourself to me. Thank You for all You have done. I rejoice in

You Lord, and all who You are!"

"And Lord I thank You for Your Precious Blood that was shed for me. I honor Your Blood, Lord Jesus, Your holy, Life-giving Blood. Thank You that Your Blood cleanses, saves, heals, and protects. Thank You for all that it does and all that it provides. Jesus, I honor Your precious Blood, and esteem it holy and pure. I praise You Lord, and celebrate the gift of Your powerful Blood."

Jesus Christ has forever changed our present earthly lives, and He has established and secured for us a glorious future. We can never run out of reasons to thank Him for His incredible sacrifice on our behalf. Jesus is our faithful, loving Savior who endured all unto death to redeem us and set us free. He is worthy of our continual thanksgiving, and His Precious Blood is to be honored and celebrated always.

Ten

Believers Can Partake of Communion to:

BE RAISED UP AND RESTORED

One of the many names of God is El Elyown, which means The Most High God. God's names are full of wonderful, multi-layered meanings, and Strong's Concordance offers interesting insights regarding this one:

El Elyown, reference #5945, *means "Lofty", "Supreme", "Highest", "The Most High."* From there, Strong's directs us to reference #5927, *Alah,* which is defined as *"to cause to ascend up", "to bring up", "to raise", "to restore".*

These definitions reveal that El Elyown, The Supreme, Most High God, is also the God who raises up, restores, and causes to rise up. His power, willingness, and faithfulness to do so is clearly demonstrated in both Old and New Testament Scriptures.

God raised/raises:

The poor – Psalm 113:4-7
Those who are bowed down – Psalm 145:14
Places of decay - Isaiah 44:26
Us! - Ephesians 2:6

He restores:

Joy – Psalm 51:12
Souls – Psalm 23:3
Comfort – Isaiah 57:18
Health – Jeremiah 30:17
Years – Joel 2:25

God, in the Person of Jesus Christ, raised up and restored multitudes of people who were in need. He restored a woman with an issue of blood, and raised Jairus' daughter from the dead (Matthew 9:18-26); He restored sight to a blind man (Mark 8:25); He restored a man's withered hand (Mark 12:13); He raised up the dead son of a widow and restored him to his mother (Luke 7:12-15); He raised Lazarus from the dead (John 11:1-44). He encountered a man with an unclean spirit near the tombs of Gadara, and restored him to his right mind (Mark 5:1-7). In this passage, the unclean spirit addressed Jesus as "The Son of the Most High God". Even the demons recognized Him as "El Elyown, the One who raises up and restores."

These and countless other works of Jesus Christ are recorded in Scripture for our benefit--that we may believe, and also experience His restoring power. Jesus is the same today as He was yesterday, and just as He raised up and restored then, He does so now. Thankfully, His power is not limited to raising only the dead or only restoring sight to the blind. Jesus is able to raise up weary souls and restore hope, rekindle desolate or struggling marriages, and restore God-given dreams or assignments that have been neglected or abandoned. God is able to restore anyone or anything that has become barren or unfruitful! His Name is El Elyown, and He alone is the Source of real restoration. At Communion we can present the barren areas of our lives to Him, and trust Him to graciously raise up and restore.

> "Lord, You have given me the gift of _____ (example: teaching), and I have allowed it to lie dormant and unfruitful for a long time. I confess my laziness and neglect as sin, and ask Your forgiveness for falling short, and for not working diligently at what You have called me to do. Jesus, as I partake of these Communion elements, I open my heart and say yes to You and Your will for my life. Rekindle in me the desire to _____ (teach), and restore to me the joy and passion of serving You. Fill me up with You Lord, and help me move obediently forward to accom-

plish all that You have called me to do. Thank You El Elyown, for raising me up to do Your will."

Married couples can share Communion together and pray:

"Jesus, thank You that in You is Life, and in You is power to raise up anything barren or lifeless. Lord, we confess that we have been distracted from You, and selfish, stubborn, and unloving towards one another. We turn from our disobedience, and ask for Your forgiveness. We submit our wills to You Lord, and commit to live by Your Word and Your ways. Jesus, thank You that Your Body and Blood bring Life and wholeness to us. As we receive these Communion elements, we ask that You would restore our souls and restore our marriage. Bond our hearts together once again, and help us return wholeheartedly--spirit, soul, and body--to the lifetime covenant we made with one another. Accomplish Your work in us Lord, then help us be willing to share Your restoring, marriage-saving power with other couples in need. Thank You Most High God, for Your love and restoration."

God cares so very much about every area of our lives. Focus on Him, trust Him, and allow Him to restore the barren areas of your life. He is able to turn them into exciting, vibrant, purpose-filled destinies, for His Glory!

Additional Scripture References

Deuteronomy 32:7-14 – El Elyown raised up Israel

2 Samuel 22, esp. vs. 17-20, 49 – El Elyown raised up/restored David

Daniel 4, esp. vs. 34, 36 (NKJV) – El Elyown restored Nebuchadnezzar

Eleven

Believers Can Partake of Communion to:
INTERCEDE FOR OTHERS

To intercede, or to make intercession means:

> to pray, petition, or plead on behalf of another
>
> to make a request in favor of another
>
> to mediate between conflicting parties with the purpose of reconciliation
>
> to put oneself between or pass between, for the benefit of another
>
> to stand in the gap for another
>
> to intervene on another's behalf.

There are many examples of intercession in the Bible - memorable accounts of God's people standing in the gap for others, sometimes even to the point of confessing another's sins. The earnest prayers and petitions of these intercessors often followed their times of intimate fellowship (communion) with God, and God responded to their intercessions with grace, deliverance, and power.

- In Genesis 18:1-8, 22-33, the Lord stayed behind and communed with Abraham after the two angels went on down to Sodom and Gomorrah. Abraham persistently interceded for any righteous remnant in those doomed cities, and God honored his petitions and saved his nephew Lot and his family.

- In Exodus 31:18, and 32:1-14, Moses communed with God on Mt. Sinai. When he came down and saw the rebellious people, he pleaded with God on their behalf. Because of Moses' prayer, God sovereignly chose to have mercy on them.

- I Chronicles 29:10-19 records David's worship and communion with God, then his prayer afterwards for God's people and his own son Solomon. God responded with abundant prosperity for Solomon and Israel.

Other examples of intercession:

> Moses prayed for Miriam's healing - Numbers 12:11-13

Ezra confessed the iniquities of God's people – Ezra 9:5-15, 10:1

Nehemiah confessed the sins of the children of Israel – Nehemiah 1:4-11

The believing centurion petitioned Jesus for the healing of his servant – Matthew 8:5-10

The good Samaritan intervened on behalf of a wounded man – Luke 10:30-35

Believers interceded for Peter's protection and deliverance – Acts 12:5-17

Paul labored in prayer for the maturity of the church in Galatia – Galatians 4:19

God answered the petitions of these faithful intercessors by clearly moving in the lives of those they mediated for and presented to Him. Intercession is obviously God's idea, and He sends His heavenly power and divine will in response to the petitions and pleas of the intercessor.

The Greatest Intercessor

The greatest act of intercession ever was the sacrificial death of Jesus Christ. Jesus willingly stood in the gap for all mankind as He hung on the cross to pay for our sins. I Peter 3:18 (NIV) reads,

> *"For Christ died for sins once for all, the righteous for the unrighteous, to bring you to God…"*

Isaiah 53:12b says,

> *"… He has poured out His soul unto death: and He was numbered with the transgressors; and He bore the sin of many, and made intercession for the transgressors."*

First Timothy 2:1, 3-6a in the Living Bible reads,

> *"… Pray much for others; plead for God's mercy upon them; give thanks for all he is going to do for them… v. 3 This is good and pleases God our Savior, for he longs for all to be saved and to understand this truth: that God is on one side and all the people on the other side, and Christ Jesus, himself man, is between them to bring them together, by giving his life for all mankind."*

The *"giving his life for all mankind"* was Jesus Christ on the cross, standing in the gap by sacrificing His own Body and Blood to bring God and man together. God's response to Christ's intercession was the provision of salvation, healing, peace, deliverance, protection, cleansing, hope, comfort, guidance, grace, victory, etc., for everyone who would believe in Him.

Intercession With Communion

Jesus' Body and Blood still mediate for mankind today; they have never lost their interceding, reconciling power. Now, as Christ's followers, our assignment is to continue to employ and wield the power of His sacrificed Body and Blood to impact the hearts and lives of people all over the earth. We are to pray continually for others, presenting them to God and asking Him to grant them the benefits and blessings that Christ has provided. God longs to reach every person with the saving, life-giving power of Jesus Christ, and He eagerly waits for and earnestly welcomes our intercessions.

Our private times of fellowship and communion with God are ideal opportunities to offer up our petitions and prayers for others. We can pray for others during our Communion time, asking God to minister to them and touch their lives. Although we cannot *take Communion for* someone else, we *can* intercede for them and present them to God as we ourselves partake.

We must always remember to examine ourselves prior to taking Communion (I Corinthians 11:27), and always acknowledge and give honor to Jesus Christ our Savior (Luke 22:19). Then, as we fellowship with God, we can pray:

> Father, Your Word says that it pleases You when we pray for others, so I take this opportunity to intercede for _____

(example: my family). I stand in the gap for my family and ask that You would touch their lives today with Jesus Christ. You sent Jesus to die for them and Your desire is for them to believe and receive the sacrifice He made on their behalf. Father, these Communion elements represent that sacrifice, and as I partake, I ask that You would minister the saving power of Christ's Blood and the healing power of His stripes to each of them. Enlighten their understanding of the truth of Jesus Christ and draw them to You. Touch their hearts, I pray, and help them give their lives to You. I commend each one of them to You Lord, and to the Word of Your grace which is able to save them. Thank You for loving them.

We can pray:

Lord, thank You for this time of fellowship with You. I love our time together! Now, Lord, as I prepare to partake of Communion this morning, I present to You and pray for _____ (example: my friend Andrew). Lord, You have placed a great calling on Andrew's life, and he has chosen to obey that call. I pray that You would reach into his life today and encourage him, strengthen him, and make his way clear. Remind him of Your faithfulness in the past, and that by Your Spirit in him he is equipped for the future. Lord, allow these life-giving elements to minister to Andrew the peace, protection, and provision that Your Body and Blood have purchased for him. Fill his heart and soul with praise and with the boldness of the Holy Spirit as he moves forward in obedience to You. Thank You for loving him, guiding him, and empowering him to do all that You have called him to do.

God has entrusted us with the great mantle of intercession, and when we are faithful to pray and stand in the gap for a person, a city, or a nation—with or without Communion—He is faithful to respond to our petitions with the limitless power and provisions of Jesus Christ, the Greatest Intercessor of all.

Twelve

Believers Can Partake of Communion to:

FELLOWSHIP WITH ONE ANOTHER

Fellowship among God's people is one of His greatest blessings to His children. Fellowship means community, communication, and it conveys the concept of "gathering together," "oneness," and "unity."

God desires fellowship and unity among His people for several reasons. One major reason is because our fellowship and unity are witnesses of His love for the world, and of the salvation He sent to mankind through Jesus Christ. Jesus Himself prayed to the Father that those who followed Him, then and now, would walk in oneness and unity. John 17:21-23 (TLB) reads,

> *"My prayer for all of them is that they will be of one heart and mind, just as you and I are, Father—that just as you are in me and I am*

> *in you, so they will be in us, and the world will believe you sent me. I have given them the glory you gave me—the glorious unity of being one, as we are—I in them and you in me, all being perfected into one—so that the world will know you sent me and will understand that you love them as much as you love me."*

Another vital reason God wants His people to fellowship is because we belong to one another. Believers joined together make up the *Body* of Christ. We are His eyes and ears, His hands and feet, His voice, and His heart of love and compassion to the whole world. Romans 12:5 says,

> *"So we being many, are one body in Christ, and everyone members of one another."*

Another important reason for believers to fellowship is because God promises Life and blessing to those who live in unity. Psalm 133:1 and 3 read,

> *"Behold, how good and how pleasant it is for brethren to dwell together in unity! v. 3 ... for there (in unity) the Lord commanded the blessing, even life forever more."*
> (Words in parentheses added for clarity.)

God wants His people to fellowship because our oneness and unity invite His Presence, and facilitate the operation of the Holy Spirit. Many times in the Old Testament when God's people gathered together for prayer, repentance, worship, or celebration, the glory of God came down, and wonderful things happened as He manifested Himself to them. In the New Testament, the early churches are described as "*... assembled together ... house to house ... with one accord ... one heart, one soul ... all things common...*" It's no wonder that we also see woven into these same passages, "*... great power ... great grace ... filled with the Holy Ghost ... boldness ... many signs and wonders*"...etc. In both Old and New Testaments, as God's people fellowshipped together and walked in unity, faith, and obedience to Him, He showed up again and again, with glorious, miraculous results!

For us, the people of God, taking Communion together is perfect fellowship. I Corinthians 10:16, 17 (NKJV) reads,

> *"The cup of blessing which we bless, is it not the communion of the blood of Christ? The bread which we break, is it not the communion of the body of Christ? For we, though many, are one bread and one body; for we all partake of that one bread."*

At Communion time, we gather together to honor Jesus Christ and celebrate the complete and flawless salvation He has provided for us. We call on His name together, confess our sins, and receive His forgiveness and cleansing. We commit our lives to Him, individually, and also united as one in Him. Then together we experience His power and Presence as He moves affectionately through our midst, touching our lives and bonding us together. Our gathering together for fellowship and Communion is God's insightful, purposeful plan and desire for His people, and our oneness and unity greatly please His huge, holy, gracious, loving heart.

When you gather together with a group of believers to partake of Communion:

- Remember Jesus Christ and the great sacrifice He made for your personal salvation, and for the salvation of the entire human race.

- Remember your church, the local body of believers that God has joined you to. Your local church has been assembled by God to accomplish a particular work for His Kingdom. Pray for your pastor and the leadership, pray for unity and harmony between members, and pray for every member to be receptive and obedient to the will and calling of God.

- Remember the corporate Church, God's people all over the earth, every race, color, nation, and tongue, united into one complete Body, with Jesus Christ the Head over all. Recognize that God has called the Church to be separate and distinct from the world, and pray as Jesus prayed: "that we may be made perfect in one." (John 17:23)

God calls for His people to fellowship with one another, and whether we gather together for worship, prayer, Communion, Bible study, social functions, or business, He wants and loves to manifest His Presence among us. Our fellowship and unity strengthen, empower, and equip us, the Body of Christ, to fulfill the work that Jesus gave us to do: "Go therefore and make disciples of all the nations…" (Matthew 28:19 NKJV)

***

This chapter is written in loving memory of my beloved pastor of 16 years, Douglas W. Graves, Word of Faith Center, Kennewick, Washington. Pastor Doug loved Communion, and passionately, tirelessly taught the importance of fellowship and unity in the Body of Christ, believing God's Word, forgiving others, and allowing the sacrificed Body and Blood of Jesus Christ to make us whole in every way. Pastor Doug was a strong believer in reaching the lost, and was faithfully dedicated to raising up leaders according to 2 Timothy 2:2:

> *"For you must teach others those things you and many others have heard me speak about. Teach these great truths to trustworthy men who will, in turn, pass them on to others." (TLB)*

Thank you Pastor Doug.
Pastor Doug Graves, 1955 - 2007

EPILOGUE

It is important for every believer to understand and remember that Communion is never to be viewed or approached as a magic wand that can be waved for instant results. Like many of the teachings of God, it takes time and study to understand it, and to learn to live in the fullness of its benefits and power.

The ministries of the Blood of Jesus alone are manifold, and understood only as we study God's Word and allow the Holy Spirit to reveal to us the depths of its meaning and power. Adding the breaking of bread, the honoring of the Lord, and prayer, for the full exercise of Communion, presents even more to learn and comprehend. I believe, however, that as you begin to incorporate Communion into your private prayer time, the Holy Spirit will increase your understanding more and more about the ministry, the joy, and the authority of ***The Body and the Blood: The Power of Communion.***

Salvation Prayer

To my unsaved relatives and friends, I have prayed continually for you, and pray even now that the reading of this book has moved your heart to believe and receive the unconditional love and gracious salvation of Almighty God through Jesus Christ.

Jesus has paid for your sins and purchased your salvation by sacrificing His Body and Blood on the cross. It is now up to you to receive that salvation, which includes the gift of abundant, eternal Life. The Bible says in Romans 10:9, 10, and 13 (NKJV),

> *" ... if you confess with your mouth the Lord Jesus and believe in your heart that God has raised Him from the dead, you will be saved. For with the heart one believes unto righteousness, and with the mouth confession is made*

unto salvation." v. 13: *"For whoever calls upon the name of the LORD shall be saved."*

A sincere prayer, spoken from your heart, will save you and make you a child of God:

> **"Jesus, I call upon Your Name right now. I believe that You died on the cross to pay for my sin, and that God raised You up again from the dead. I ask You to come into my heart and be my Savior and the Lord of my life. Forgive me for every sin, wash me clean, and fill me up to overflowing with You. I give You my life, Jesus, and I choose to live for You always. I let go of all my past and commit my future to You. Thank You, Jesus, for loving me enough to die for me. Thank You for saving me, and thank You, Lord, that I now belong to You. Amen."**

If you prayed this prayer, welcome to the family of God! I encourage you to seek out a Bible-believing, Bible-teaching church where you can fellowship with like believers and be taught to live in all that God has for you.

May this book be only the beginning of your new life and journey with Jesus Christ, and may your understanding and celebration of the power of His Body and Blood gloriously transform your life, and make all things new. The blessings of the Lord and King of heaven and earth await you!

TO GOD BE ALL THE GLORY!

A Note of Transparency from the Author

Dear Reader:

We know that although we are followers of Jesus Christ, we are not exempt from life's hardships and difficulties. God allows us to experience tough, uncertain times to draw us to Himself, to teach us to trust Him, and to reveal to us what we're really made of. Also, we have an adversary whose sinister goal is to derail us, discourage us, and destroy our lives.

Throughout the writing of this book, I experienced numerous trials and difficulties: the loss of my father, my twin sister, and my pastor of 16 years; job loss; several serious health issues; and most recently--the challenge and stress of learning a new and extremely complex job. Needless to say,

I've had plenty of opportunities to use the material in this book.

By God's unwavering grace, I have been able to endure these trying, often overwhelming times, and through it all I can truthfully say that God is faithful, and His Word and promises are true.

To those of you who know, worship, and work with me, you've probably seen me at my best and at my worst. Thank you for loving me anyway in my imperfect state, and for keeping me continually in your prayers. I am forever grateful to you.

God's Greatest Blessing (aka Jesus Christ) to you all.

Lavonne

About the Author

Lavonne Baker is a native and long-time resident of Washington State. After earning a Bachelor degree in Sociology/Social Work at Washington State University, she moved to California where she lived, worked, and attended church for 13 years. She returned to Washington in 1989, completed 18 months of Bible School, and, at the insistent prompting of the Holy Spirit, she began to compile the teachings He had given her about Communion.

It was during Lavonne's private devotional times that the Holy Spirit began to teach her that God wants our Communion times, whether individual or with fellow believers, to be Holy Spirit-directed, full of meaning, and life-changing.

Recommendation by Ryan D. Graves

The Body and the Blood: The Power of Communion, has no doubt unfolded a incredible picture and has unpacked revelation and insight to the power of communion. It explores with depth the power of the cross and the covenant we have with the Lord which was ratified by the Blood of Jesus. It lays the foundation as being more than a religious ordinance that we do from time to time but rather the intimacy and covenant we now share with the Lord.

Through this material the body of Christ can rightly discern the blood and the Body of Christ, and can experience in their lives healing blessing and transformation.

~ *Ryan D. Graves, Senior Pastor, Word of Faith Center, Kennewick, WA*